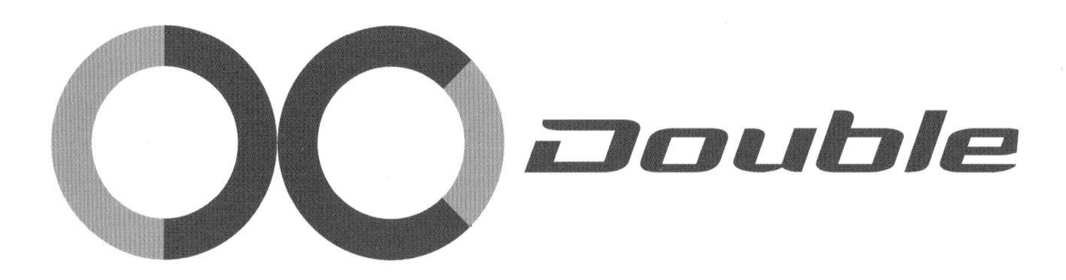

ENGLISH
Pupil Book 2

Tom Watt
with
Gillian Howell

Rising Stars UK Ltd, 22 Grafton Street, London W1S 4EX

www.risingstars-uk.com

Published 2008

Story author: Tom Watt
Educational author: Gillian Howell
Publisher: Gill Budgell
Cover design: Burville-Riley Partnership
Design and project management: Cambridge Publishing Management
Illustrations: Patrick Boyer, for Illustration, Ltd
Photographs: Getty Images

British Library Cataloguing in Publication Data.
A CIP record for this book is available from the British Library.

ISBN: 978-1-84680-299-7

Printed by: Craftprint International Ltd, Singapore

Rising Stars would like to thank Alan Sefton and Scott Cohen of Football in the Community for Arsenal Football Club for their help and support.

Contents

Stuart Dolan
Year 7

Homework Topic
My Dream

My grandad is always saying he can remember when Shelby Town were just an amateur team. There were only a couple of blokes and a dog who used to watch them play, and the dog usually got bored and went off chasing rabbits! But Grandad would stick around till the end. He told people that Shelby would have a proper team and a proper ground one day and that he'd take his grandchildren to watch them play against Man United and Liverpool.

That's why I've been going to watch Town since I was four years old. Me, Grandad and Mum never miss a game. Maybe I would have loved football anyway but I think Grandad has had a lot to do with it. I play for my school team and for the Cubs. I play in the garden, up the park, on the beach when we go on holiday to our caravan. I love football more than anything else and my greatest ambition is to play for Shelby Town FC.

I know millions of boys want to be footballers. Maybe they want to earn lots of money, be seen on TV and drive flash cars. I know that football is very competitive and that very few boys get the chance to play for a professional team, even the ones who are good players when they are young. But that's not going to stop me trying.

I watch the Shelby players every week at Manor Park. I watch all the top Premiership players on Sky as well. I don't know if I could ever be one of them but I'm going to try as hard as I can to get as far as I can. My dream is just to have the chance, even if it's only once, to run out of the tunnel and play for Shelby Town, and I want Grandad to be there to see me do it.

Team Talk:

- Talk about how much Stuart was influenced by his grandad.
- In terms of football, who has influenced you most?

Skills Practice 1

Change these past-tense sentences to the present tense and then to the future tense.

a) Shelby Town were just an amateur team.
b) The supporters were mostly friends and family.
c) The players weren't professionals.

Skills Practice 2

Change this present-tense sentence to the past tense.

a) I don't know if I could ever be one of them but I'm going to try as hard as I can to get as far as I can.

Change this past-tense sentence to the future tense.

b) Manchester City achieved greater success when they moved to the City of Manchester Stadium.

Game On

Answer these questions with full sentences.

1. Which two clubs did Grandad want his grandchildren to watch Shelby Town play?
2. How old was Stuart when he first went to watch Shelby Town?
3. How does Stuart think he differs from the millions of other boys who want to be footballers?
4. Why does Stuart want his grandad to see him run out of the tunnel at Shelby Town?
5. Grandad said that only a couple of blokes and a dog used to watch Shelby Town. Does he really mean this? Write a sentence explaining his meaning.

SPORT January 15th • *Shelby Gazette*

SHELBY BOY SMASHES GOAL-SCORING RECORD

Mum, teachers, pals 'really proud'

Last Thursday was an afternoon to remember for everybody connected with Osborne School in Shelby. And extra special for one young man in particular: under-12 star striker Stuart Dolan.

Leeside Schools under-12s is a friendly league but if there was a table there's no doubt who'd be top of it! Osborne's 4-1 win over Aniston Park on Thursday was their 12th in a row. The two goals scored by Stuart Dolan were his 24th and 25th of the season. That's an average of two goals per game, a record Michael Owen would be proud of!

After the game, the *Gazette* spoke to Stuart's form teacher, Mr Pritchard, who runs the Osborne under-12 team:

'Stuart's a very nice lad and we're proud of him. He scores the goals but he's a real team player.'

No wonder Stuart's popular with his team-mates, according to Mr Pritchard:

'We've never had an under-12 team at Osborne before, but Stuart and his pals came to see me at the start of term. They were so keen, I couldn't say no to the idea! We haven't looked back since.'

On Thursday, Stuart scored one with his head and one from outside the box with a right-foot shot. His mother, Jenny Dolan, says she's not surprised the team's done so well:

'I'm really proud of all of them. Stuart and his friends just play football every minute they can. I don't know how good they are, but I know they have a fantastic time playing for the school.'

Well, if this season is anything to go by, we'd say Osborne under-12s – and star striker Stuart Dolan – are looking very good indeed! Remember that name. Who knows? Stuart Dolan and his pals might be Premier League players in the making!

Team Talk:

- Find the verbs that tell you this is a recount of an event.
- Is your team made up of 'real team players'?

Skills Practice 1

Choose the best time-adverb for the spaces in the sentences below.

Initially *At first* *Finally*
In the end *Later* *Soon*

a) _____ the team were swamped by the attacking forwards.
b) _____ they substituted a defender.
c) _____ the play swung in their favour.

Skills Practice 2

Rewrite these sentences by moving the underlined phrases to another position in the sentence.

a) <u>After the game</u>, the *Gazette* spoke to Stuart's form teacher.
b) Stuart and his pals came to see me <u>at the start of term.</u>
c) <u>On Thursday</u>, Stuart scored one with his head and one from outside the box with a right-foot shot.

Write a time-based adverbial phrase to complete this sentence.

_____ Fulham were thought to be the underdogs.

Game On

Answer these questions with full sentences.

Manager's Message
Adverbs can be single words or phrases.
Adverbs of time tell us when something happens.

1. What team does Stuart play for?
2. When was the team first formed?
3. How many goals had Stuart scored before this game?
4. How does Stuart's mother feel about the team? Give a reason for your answer.
5. What does Mr Pritchard mean when he says, 'He scores the goals but he's a real team player'?

Match-day programme Shelby Town v Preston North End, May 5, Kick-off 3.00

May 5

The Diamond vision

First of all, I'd like to welcome the players, officials and supporters of Preston North End. They have had a really good season and we wish them all the best in the Championship play-offs. I think their manager, Billy Davies, is going to make a big name for himself in the future.

I'd also like to say thank you to all our supporters here at Manor Park. It hasn't been easy for us this season, but nobody thought it would be. It's a big jump between League One and the Championship and I think the boys have done really well to adapt.

We don't have as much money to spend as the big clubs in this division. Back in August, I told the team that staying up was going to be the target. Thanks to the win at Leicester last week we've done that now. The lads have worked really hard and your support has made a big difference.

Like you, I hope that one day it'll be us pushing for a place in the Premier League. As I say though, we won't be able to buy our way to promotion. The team we have now is a good mix of young lads who haven't made it at other clubs and more experienced players who still have something to prove.

In the future, I expect us to start producing more of our own players. There are plenty of youngsters around Shelby and Leeside who we're looking at. We have to make sure the best ones don't go off to join big clubs. Town are a Championship side now and I hope local lads will want to come and play for our Academy.

We have a great team behind the scenes on the youth side, led by Derek Hardaker. Derek and his staff have made our Academy as professional as any around. I think we have a proper system now for bringing young players through at Manor Park. I hope those local boys will end up being Shelby Town's stars of the future!

Up the Town! *Mick Diamond*

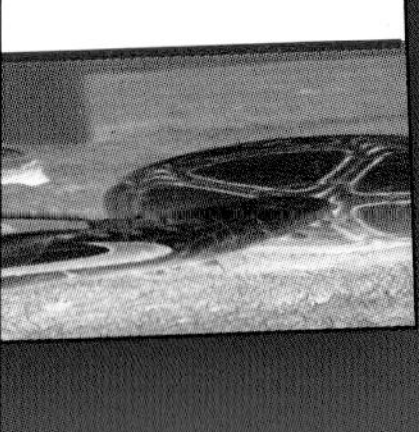

Team Talk:

- Which league are Shelby Town playing in? How can you tell?
- Which league does your team play in?

Skills Practice 1

Choose the correct word endings for these pairs of words.

a) divition/division
b) promotion/promosion
c) evolusion/evolution

Skills Practice 2

Practise spelling these words using Look Say Cover Write Check.

a) vision
b) collision
c) occasion
d) solution
e) revolution
f) relation
g) nation

Fill in the missing word with a *-tion* or *-sion* ending.

Newcastle United's midfielder will be out of _____ following injury.

Game On

Answer these questions with full sentences.

1. Who are Shelby Town playing against in this match?
2. What sort of players make up the Shelby Town team?
3. Why has it been a difficult season for Shelby Town?
4. How do Shelby Town intend to produce young players of their own?
5. What is the purpose of Mick Diamond's message?

Bob Ferris opened the door to the dressing room and let Stuart walk inside.

'Lads, say hello to our new striker. Stuart Dolan, meet the Shelby Dynamos!'

As the door closed behind him, Stuart looked round the room. His new team-mates were all changed and ready for the evening's training session. A couple of them nodded their heads in his direction. Most of them just stared at him, as if to say, 'What's this kid here for?'

When Mr Ferris had phoned Mum and asked if he'd like to come along to train with the Dynamos, Stuart had said yes straight away. It was only after Mum had put the phone down that he'd started to have second thoughts. He knew about the Dynamos. Everybody did. They were the best junior team for miles around. It was great to be asked to join them. But it was scary as well.

All the boys in the dressing room were at least two years older than him. The Dynamos played in the Leeside under-16 league, after all. Looking at them now, as they looked at him, a couple of his new team-mates seemed almost like grown men. Mr Ferris had told Stuart not to worry. He'd told him he had enough ability to compete against older boys, and Stuart wanted to believe him. Right now though, standing in the dressing room with no one saying a word, he wasn't so sure.

Finally, Mr Ferris broke the ice.

'Stuart is the best finisher I've ever seen at his age, boys. He might be a titch, but if you get the ball to him in the box, he'll do the rest. If we look out for him then he'll win games for us, I guarantee you.'

At last, one of the boys stood up. He was a good foot taller than Stuart, as he reached out for a handshake.

'Well, if Mr Ferris thinks you're any good then you must be. Otherwise he'd have to be wrong about the rest of us, too, wouldn't he?'

Mr Ferris laughed, and so did the rest of the boys.

'I'm Matt. I'm captain of Shelby Dynamos. Welcome to the team. You'd better hang your stuff on that hook over there.'

Team Talk:
- Choose one word to say how Stuart felt.
- Who is the smallest player in your team?

Skills Practice 1

Look through the text and find all the words with 'ea' vowel patterns. Group them according to the sound they make, like this:

/e/	ready,
/ee/	
/ay/	

Skills Practice 2

Write a single sentence using each of these 'ai' words once.

captain said against straight training

How many spellings of the long 'a' vowel sound can you find in this sentence?

Southampton FC, nicknamed The Saints, play at St Mary's Stadium and were relegated to the Championship after playing at the top for 27 years.

Game On

Answer these questions with full sentences.

1. What is Stuart's new team called?
2. What is the team captain called?
3. Why did most of the team stare at Stuart?
4. What did Mr Ferris mean when he said, 'Stuart is the best finisher'?
5. What do you think Stuart's 'second thoughts' were?

Shelby Dynamos FC

Shelby Dynamos FC
24 Balcolm Drive
Shelby
Leeside

Dear Parents,

I am delighted that you have agreed to your son joining Shelby Dynamos for this summer's international tournament. The Kappa Junior Cup will be taking place in Arnhem in Holland between the 2nd and the 7th of August. It will be a great opportunity for the boys to play against top teams from other parts of Europe. I am sure they will enjoy themselves, and who knows, we might even bring the Cup back to Shelby!

The lads will get at least one game at the stadium in Arnhem, which is a proper 25,000-seater UEFA standard ground. They tell me the pitch there slides in and out under the stands so it can get plenty of sun and air. Not while a game is going on, though! During our stay, we will play at least one game every day. The people running the Cup say we will face one or two local Dutch teams and also teams from France, Spain, Portugal and Sweden. It will be a great experience.

I will be in touch nearer the time with the details of the trip. I can tell you we will be travelling by minibus to Harwich and then taking the ferry to Hook of Holland. The tournament organisers will lay on transport to Arnhem from there. We will leave Shelby early on the morning of the 1st of August and be back on the afternoon of August 8th. The boys will be staying in student flats while we are in Holland and will, of course, be supervised by myself and Mrs Ferris at all times.

Finally, the painful bit! As you know, we are paying for the team's accommodation and meals in Holland from club funds. Parents have agreed to pay for the team's travel expenses. I must put down a deposit with the travel agent next week. Could you let me have a cheque or cash for £25 at the game on Sunday?

Thanks for your support,

Bob Ferris

(Manager)

Shelby Dynamos FC

Team Talk:

- Look at each paragraph. Why has the writer begun a new paragraph each time?
- Have you ever played abroad? Would you like to? What do you think it would be like?

Skills Practice 1

Add the suffix *-ing* to these verbs.

a) travel
b) stay
c) score
d) ensure
e) refer
f) dribble

Check your answers with the text.

Manager's Message
Take care of your spelling when adding the suffix *-ing* to a verb. Learn the rules about doubling consonants and dropping the final 'e'.

Skills Practice 2

Rewrite the following sentences and add exclamation marks or question marks as appropriate.

a) I am delighted your son will be joining us
b) Will we bring back the Cup
c) The pitch doesn't slide during games
d) It will be a great experience
e) Now for the painful bit
f) Can you send a cheque by Friday

Add the correct punctuation and capitals to this sentence.

manchester uniteds under-18s emerged winners of the pele challenge cup watched by the brazilian legend himself

Game On

Answer these questions with full sentences.

1. Where will the Kappa Junior Cup take place?
2. How many games will the team play each day?
3. Why does the pitch slide in and out?
4. On what dates will the first and last matches be played?
5. Why does Mr Ferris call the last paragraph 'the painful bit'?

August 2004

7 Thursday

Well, we didn't quite make it. The semi-final last night was a really good game. The team we played against was from Lyon in France. They had a giant playing at centre half so it wasn't much good me going up with him for headers. But I still got a goal. Frank Jennings got a cross in from the right and I managed to poke my toe out and deflect it past their keeper.

They were winning 2-0 by then and we were all out attacking. They got another couple in the second half and we ended up losing 4-2. Mr Ferris said he was very pleased with us. He had been talking to some of the other coaches during the game. They had said how well we passed the ball. One of them said it was a pity the England team didn't play like us!

So today we have one more game before we go home. It's the 3rd and 4th place play-off. We will be playing at the Vitesse Arnhem Stadium. It's a proper Dutch League ground and we are playing against one of the local teams. That means there will be a big crowd. Not 25,000, but still more people than I've ever played in front of before!

We've had a great time here. The rooms are nice and clean and the football has been great. I'm glad I shared a room with Tony Moore. He's been playing for Dynamos for a year and a half, but I didn't really know him all that well. We have made friends this week even though he's a Spurs supporter. I keep telling him that, one day, Shelby will be playing in the Premiership against Paul Robinson, Robbie Keane and all the other Tottenham stars.

I'm glad I have started keeping this diary as well. Everything is happening so quickly. It will be good to be able to look back and remember everything that has happened at this tournament. Especially if we win the 3rd place trophy later today!

Team Talk:

- Why is Stuart glad he started a diary?
- What sort of things would you write in a football diary for your team?

Skills Practice 1

Look through Stuart's diary entry and write down all the adjectives you can find.

Skills Practice 2

Change the adjectives in these sentences to more interesting ones.

a) The semi-final last night was a really good game.
b) Mr Ferris said he was very pleased with us.
c) That means there will be a big crowd.
d) The rooms are nice and clean and the football has been great.

Choose adjectives to make this sentence more interesting.

Portsmouth are looking for _____ players to boost the team's _____ performance.

Game On

Answer these questions with full sentences.

1. Who did Shelby Dynamos play in the semi-final?
2. Who did Stuart share a room with?
3. Why was Mr Ferris pleased with the team?
4. Why does Stuart write '*even though* he's a Spurs supporter'?
5. If Stuart became a famous footballer, to what use could he put his diary?

Rob Mills (Presenter): Thanks, Emma. More travel coming up in half an hour on BBC Radio Leeside. Back to our phone-in feature now. Remember you can call any time on 01929 700600 and be part of the show. We're talking about getting kids off the street and involved in something worthwhile. And we're joined now by Bob Ferris, the Manager of Shelby Dynamos FC. Hi, Bob.

Bob Ferris: Hello, Rob. Thanks for having me on.

Rob Mills: So you're doing your bit to keep local kids out of trouble?

Bob Ferris: Well, not really. I just run a football team for lads who love playing. It's not a charity or anything.

Rob Mills: No, but playing for the team keeps them out of trouble, doesn't it?

Bob Ferris: I don't know. I don't think my lads would be doing any mischief anyway. They'd be more likely at home or something. I think people have the wrong idea about youngsters anyway. They see more than two lads out on the street together and straight away think they're up to no good.

Rob Mills: Isn't that true, though?

Bob Ferris: No, of course not. Most kids I know just want to be with their mates and have something to do. The ones who like football can come and play for the Dynamos.

Rob Mills: Any stars of the future there, Bob?

Bob Ferris: Well, who knows? I think we've had one or two scouts from pro clubs along to our games in the past few months. The boys did really well in a tournament in Holland over the summer. Maybe the word's getting round! It's more about them enjoying themselves and enjoying football though, really.

Rob Mills: Great, Bob.

Bob Ferris: Thanks, Rob.

Rob Mills: Sounds like they're having a fantastic time. It's been great talking to you. That's Bob Ferris, Manager of Shelby Dynamos. Time now for you to have your say on BBC Radio Leeside. Call 01929 700600. This is Thora from Shelby Park. Hello, Thora. What have you got to say?

Team Talk:

- Retell the main points of the interview using the comic strip as a prompt.
- Why might some people think you are up to no good when you are out with your mates?

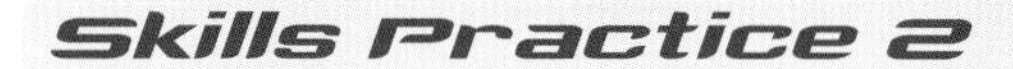

Skills Practice 1

Practise spelling these words using Look Say Cover Write Check.

a) travel
b) local
c) trouble
d) people
e) devil
f) legal

Skills Practice 2

Add the correct speech punctuation to these sentences.

a) Hello Rob said Bob Thanks for having me on.
b) Are you doing your bit to keep kids out of trouble asked Rob.
c) Well he replied Playing football helps doesn't it?
d) I think he added that people have the wrong idea about kids.
e) Isn't that true though asked Rob.

Read this sentence. Identify any words you might have trouble spelling and practise them.

The Middlesbrough players had another frustrating match and, although they had many chances, were not being ruthless enough in attack.

Game On

Answer these questions with full sentences.

1. What is the name of the radio station?
2. What is the phone-in feature about?
3. What is the name of the radio station's travel reporter?
4. What is Bob Ferris's opinion about youngsters?
5. What does Bob mean when he says 'the word's getting round'?

Player Report/Confidential

Player name: **Stuart Dolan**
Date of birth: **23 March, 1990**
Nationality: **British (Shelby)**
Position: **Striker**
Height: **1.60m**

Stuart Dolan has been watched by Frank Hooper and myself several times over the past few weeks. He has been playing up front for Shelby Dynamos. Yesterday we watched him against Leeside Express at Manningham Park in the Leeside Junior District League. Dolan scored twice against Leeside, Dynamos winning the game 3-1. The team is playing at under-16 level. Dolan himself is 14 years old.

Analysis

Strengths: Dolan looks like an out-and-out goalscorer in the mould of a Michael Owen or an Andy Johnson. Very alert, very quick off the mark. Although physically much smaller than his team-mates and the opposition, the boy looked comfortable. Took his goals well: one close-range finish with his right foot from a cross, one right-foot shot from the edge of the penalty area. Brave in every physical challenge and willing to track back whenever his team lost the ball. Excellent first touch and close control.

Weaknesses: Obviously Dolan still has a lot of growing to do. When the ball is played into his feet during open play, bigger boys are able to out-muscle him and win possession. Tends not to be aware of his options when he is involved in build-up play. Selfish in and around the penalty area, but then was there ever a good striker who wasn't? Did most of his best work early in the game, and tired second half. Substituted on 60 minutes.

Recommendation

I think Dolan is definitely worth a look at Manor Park. His manager, Bob Ferris, says he's a lovely lad and a very willing worker who wants to learn. Even against boys a couple of years older than he is, Dolan was a real handful. May well be one of those players who scores goals at any level. I recommend we invite him to train with our under-16s.

Henry Whittingham

Henry Whittingham (Youth Scout)

Team Talk:

- What are two of Stuart's strengths and two of his weaknesses?
- What are two of your own football strengths and weaknesses?

Skills Practice 1

Change these adjectives into nouns by adding the suffix *-ness*.
Write them down.

a) alert
b) close
c) selfish
d) good
e) lovely

Skills Practice 2

Change these irregular adjectives into nouns.

a) strong
b) real
c) beautiful
d) dangerous
e) odd
f) long

Which adjectives could you change into nouns in this sentence?
Rewrite the new sentence.
Write the correct nouns.

A simple pass up the line, followed by an accurate cross, resulted in the best goal of the season.

Game On

Answer these questions with full sentences.

1. Who were Shelby Dynamos playing when the report was written?
2. What position does Stuart play?
3. What are the names of the scouts who watched Stuart?
4. Why could bigger boys win possession from Stuart?
5. Does the scout think that Stuart's selfishness in the penalty area is really a weakness? Refer to the text to support your answer.

TV

Gerald Sanford: Thanks, Jenny. Yes, something a little different on Leeside Sport this evening. Let's forget all about that defeat at The Hawthorns for Shelby Town on Saturday. We're at the indoor facility at Manor Park and, for once, we're not here to get the latest from Mick Diamond. Look behind me and you'll see coaches and boys hard at work. It's evening training for Town hopefuls between the ages of 11 and 16. Let's see if we can grab a word with one of them. Hello. What's your name, young man? Good goal you smacked in a minute ago!

Stuart: Yeah, thanks. Well, it was a good pass from Terry, actually.

Gerald: What was your name again?

Stuart: Oh, Stuart Dolan.

Gerald: Exciting time for you, Stuart?

Stuart: Fantastic. This is only my second time here. Mr Whittingham came round last week and told Mum that Town wanted me to train with them. I couldn't believe it!

Gerald: That'd be the Chief Scout, Henry Whittingham, wouldn't it? And who's been taking you for training?

Stuart: Mr Hardaker. He runs the whole Academy and he's been looking at us tonight. It's amazing. We've got proper changing rooms and equipment and everything. Mr Hardaker's a proper professional coach, isn't he?

Gerald: Think you'll be playing for Shelby one day?

Stuart: I don't know. I'm a Shelby Town supporter so I'm going to do the best I can.

Derek Hardaker (shouts from behind camera): Hey, Stuart, the best you can do is come over here. We're starting five-a-side and I'm sticking you in goal for a change!

Stuart: Coming, Mr Hardaker!

Gerald: Well, Jenny. There you have it. A peek behind the scenes with young Town hopeful Stuart Drummond. Back to you in the studio.

Stuart (shouts from pitch): Dolan! My name's Stuart Dolan! Which goal, Mr Hardaker?

Team Talk:

- Imagine you are Stuart and read his words aloud in an expressive voice.
- What happens at your training sessions?

Skills Practice 1

Rewrite these shortened forms of words in full.

a) let's
b) we're
c) it's
d) what's
e) couldn't
f) that'd

Skills Practice 2

Rewrite these phrases in a shortened form by replacing omitted letters with an apostrophe.

a) you will
b) would not
c) is not
d) you would
e) he had
f) does not

Find and shorten the verbs in these sentences.

The ref is looking at the linesman. He has pulled a card out. It is not red!

Game On

Answer these questions with full sentences.

1. What is the age range of the boys who are training?
2. How many times has Stuart been to training at the Academy?
3. How does Stuart feel about the facilities?
4. Find two things Stuart says that suggest he is modest about his skills.
5. Why do you think Mr Hardaker put Stuart in goal for five-a-side?

Stuart Dolan
Year 9

Homework Project
My Hero

I play football. I watch football. I think about football. Most nights, I dream about football as well! When I think of the people I admire, they all have something to do with football. Even Mum, because she is a Shelby Town supporter just like me and Grandad. Now that I am training at Manor Park twice a week, I've got new people that I look up to like Mr Hardaker and Mr Diamond.

If I was to say who my all-time hero was, though, I would say Michael Owen. Almost my first memory of football is the World Cup in France in 1998. I will always remember the goal Owen scored for England against Argentina when he ran from the halfway line and then smashed it in. He was not much older than I am now! But he was so fast and so brave. I couldn't believe it! Even though he was a Liverpool player, I said I was going to watch everything he did in his career.

I've watched him play for Liverpool, Real Madrid, Newcastle and England. He's achieved so many things already in his career and I'm sure he'll win more trophies before he's finished. You can talk about the goals he scored to win the Cup against Arsenal, about his goals in Spain when nobody thought he would even get a game, about him scoring one every two games for England. The thing that I most admire about Owen, though, is what he is like when things go wrong.

He has had a lot of injuries but he always comes back and proves he can still do the business. I remember when he got his knee injury at the World Cup in Germany. A lot of people were saying he was finished, but he came back and proved them wrong. He's small, like me. But I think Michael Owen is a very big man inside. He has got to the top by being a good player. But he has also got there by being very determined, and that's really why he's my hero.

Team Talk:
- What is the main point or focus of each paragraph?
- Who is your football hero?

Skills Practice 1

Find all the compound words in Stuart's essay. Write the whole word and then split it into its smaller words.

Skills Practice 2

Join words from the list to make compound words.

- every
- stand
- no
- foot
- body
- one
- ball
- under

Invent three new compound words about football.

Game On

Answer these questions with full sentences.

1. In the first paragraph, which four people does Stuart say he admires?
2. What is Stuart's first memory of Michael Owen?
3. What is it that Stuart most admires about Owen?
4. What does the phrase 'do the business' mean? Put it into your own words.
5. Write two ways in which Stuart might be like Michael Owen.

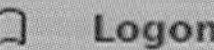

http://www.shelby.premiumtv.co.uk/

Logon Contact A Creative BBC NEWS | ... Front Page Demon Inter...Mail: Login eBay UK – T...Marketplace

Shelby Town FC

- Home
- News
- Manager's page
- Fixtures
- Match reports
- Online shop
- Contact us

TRIAL DATES ANNOUNCED FOR NEXT SEASON'S ACADEMY PLACES – ALL ENQUIRIES WELCOME!

Special Feature

Youth Supremo: The Future's Bright for Town!

Derek Hardaker came to Manor Park just weeks after Mick Diamond was appointed manager back in 2002. His job is to find tomorrow's first-team players. In an exclusive interview, Shelby Town's Academy Director tells Sandy Lane why he's optimistic about the club's future prospects.

Sandy Lane: Thanks for talking to us, Derek. We know the first team's made a good start to the season. How are things going at the Academy?

Derek Hardaker: Really well, Sandy. As you know, the Academy has only been up and running properly for six or seven years. So it's a bit early to say when we can expect to see local boys coming through. But the scholars are doing fine, and in the younger age groups we have some really promising lads at Manor Park.

Sandy: People have been getting excited about one or two of the younger boys, haven't they?

Derek: Yes, you mean lads like Stuart Dolan, don't you? Well, I don't want to put too much pressure on them. But, usually, if you get one or two prospects each year you are doing well. You have to be an Alex Ferguson to get a bunch together like United did with Beckham and Scholes and the Nevilles back in the '90s.

Sandy: What are the chances of finding a group like that for Mick Diamond?

Derek: Well, hang on. I'm not saying they will be as good as those United boys! But I think the age group who become Academy scholars next year may be the best group of young players this club has ever seen.

Sandy: So the future looks bright?

Derek: I think we'll see one or two Academy boys involved with the first team in the next couple of years. And, as I say, some of the younger ones may come through very quickly indeed. There's a lot can happen to a young player before he becomes a pro. But our boys have the right attitude to what they are doing. Fingers crossed, they'll be at the heart of Shelby Town for many years to come!

Team Talk:

- Think of three questions you would ask Derek Hardaker about the Academy.
- What would you like or dislike about attending a football academy?

Skills Practice 1

Rewrite these sentences using the words *to*, *two* or *too* to fill the spaces.

a) Thanks for talking _____ us, Derek
b) Well, I don't want _____ put _____ much pressure on them.
c) If you get one or _____ prospects each year you are doing well.
d) I think we'll see one or _____ Academy boys involved with the first team.
e) There's a lot can happen _____ a young player.

Now check your answers with the text.

Skills Practice 2

Write three sentences of your own, beginning with *to*, *two* and *too*.

Fill in the spaces in this sentence.

I am going _____ watch City play and I hope you _____ can come _____.

Game On

Answer these questions with full sentences.

1. For how long has the Academy been going?
2. What is Derek Hardaker's job?
3. Why do you think people were getting excited about one or two of the younger boys?
4. What does Derek Hardaker mean when he calls some of the lads 'promising'?
5. Derek Hardaker says he doesn't want to put too much pressure on them. What might happen if he did put too much pressure on them?

May 2004

5 Monday

Mum came with me to the club today because Derek Hardaker wanted to talk to all of us. The letter said he needed to discuss next season. It was almost like going to school to get your report or something. I was really nervous and so were the other boys, I could tell. Mum kept saying on the way down to Manor Park, 'Don't worry. Just relax. As long as you've done your best then everything will be OK.' She was telling me to calm down but when we were in the corridor outside the office, waiting, I could tell she was even more nervous than me!

Anyway, I shouldn't have worried. If I had done anything wrong, Mr Hardaker would have told me. He's a very gentle man. When he is coaching he never seems to shout or get angry. But when things don't go right, or somebody isn't paying attention, he has this way of making you stop whatever you're doing and listen. He has a look he gives you and it's scarier than if he'd lost his temper, I think! I've learnt a lot from him already, even though I've only been training with Town for ten weeks.

Anyway, we went into the office and Mr Hardaker was wearing a suit and was very polite. He said, 'Hello, Stuart. Hello, Mrs Dolan.' He told my mum that the club was really pleased with my attitude. He even said I was a credit to her! Obviously, Mum loved that! Then he said that he hoped I'd be back in July and that if there were any problems, with football or anything else, then Mum should just give him a call.

I love it at Town. I watch the game at the weekend and now, Monday and Friday, I'm training at the club! I'm starting to feel part of it even though we don't really meet the first-team players. Mum must be pleased too. She bought me a new pair of Puma Kings on the way home that she and Grandad had saved up for. I'm going down the park to try them out now!

Team Talk:
- What sort of language used tells you this is a diary entry?
- What would you write in your own diary if you were Stuart?

Skills Practice 1

Write your own definition of these words, then check them in a dictionary.

a) discuss
b) nervous
c) relax
d) calm
e) gentle
f) credit

Skills Practice 2

Choose alternative words for the underlined words in these sentences.

a) The letter said he needed to discuss next season.
b) He's a very gentle man.
c) He told my mum that the club was really pleased with my attitude.

Choose an alternative word or phrase for the underlined verb in this sentence.

The Premier League consists of the 20 top teams in the English Football Association.

Game On

Answer these questions with full sentences.

1. Where did Stuart wait before seeing Mr Hardaker?
2. How long has Stuart been training with Town?
3. Why would Stuart's mum love being told that he was a credit to her?
4. How did Stuart know his mum was pleased?
5. Describe your impression of Mr Hardaker.

Stuart knocked on the door of the headmaster's office.

'Come in!'

Stuart opened the door. The Head looked up from the paper he was working on and smiled. He pointed to a chair on the other side of the desk.

'Ah, Stuart. Thanks for coming along. Don't look so worried! There's no problem. Now you're settled in Year 10, I just wanted us to have a little chat. You know, about school and your football.'

'Yes, sir.'

'Your form teacher is very pleased with your progress. A little behind with maths, but Mr Davis says you are working hard at it. He's sure it will come in plenty of time for your GCSEs. We're very proud of what you're doing with your football and we all wish you the best of luck.'

'Thank you, Mr Sparrow.'

'I just want to make sure you understand how important it is to keep up here at Osborne. I know you have got a chance to do something you love at Shelby Town, but I don't want you to get carried away. So many boys go into football, but it doesn't work out for all of them. Maybe it will for you, but you never know. You may find yourself in two years' time or four years' time having to think again about what you're going to do with yourself. That's why it's so important you don't miss out on school and what you can achieve here. We think you can cope with A levels and go on to college if you want to. You should think very carefully about doing that. I'm going to talk to your mum about it later in the term, but I thought it would be good for us to have a chat in the meantime.'

'Yes, sir.'

'I'm sure you know what I'm saying. Don't give up on your work here at school. Football is the most important thing to you, I know. But if you do your best here at Osborne, we know you'll be prepared for whatever happens. Keep up the good work.'

'Thank you, Mr Sparrow.'

'Oh, by the way, do you know of any way I might get hold of a couple of tickets for the FA Cup game against Blackburn on Saturday?'

Team Talk:

- What is the difference between this description of Stuart meeting the headmaster and his meeting with Mr Hardaker?
- How do you feel if you have to go to see the head of your school?

Skills Practice 1

Look through the text and find words with 'ou' vowels. Group them according to their different vowel sounds, for example:

/ow/	about,
/or/	
/oo/ (book)	should,
/oo/ (zoo)	

Skills Practice 2

Write as many words as you can think of with 'ou' vowels to match the different sounds in these words.

a) your
b) you
c) would
d) round

Find all the 'ou' vowels in the following sentence. How many different ones are there?

The board at Fulham has released a thought-provoking announcement about four new signings.

Game On

Answer these questions with full sentences.

1. In which subject does Stuart need to catch up?
2. What is the headmaster's name?
3. Why does the headmaster tell Stuart to keep up his work at school?
4. What does the headmaster think Stuart might be able to do in the future?
5. Write a sentence to say what the purpose of the Head's talk was.

Shelby Town FC

24 Balcolm Drive
Shelby
Leeside

March 24

Dear Mrs Dolan,

It was very nice to meet up with you at the game last Saturday. We all hope you, Stuart and your father enjoyed the afternoon. It was a good win for the first team against Queens Park Rangers. I think people are starting to realise this is a club moving forward now. I very much enjoyed speaking to your dad about the old days. A reminder of how far we have already come!

I'm sure you know how delighted we are with the progress Stuart has made with our under-16s this season. This letter will probably come as no surprise.

I am writing to offer Stuart a place as a scholar at the Shelby Town Academy starting next August. As I explained the other day, he would be with us as an Academy player for two years. After that, we would then sit down with the first-team Manager, Mick Diamond, to talk about the possibility of a professional contract for Stuart in the future.

I know one or two other clubs, including Manchester City, have been in touch with you about Stuart. We believe that Manor Park would be the best place for your son to continue with his football education. Especially as he is a Shelby Town fan!

There are no certainties in modern football. However, we think Stuart is a real prospect. We hope he can develop into a first-team player here at the club. I can assure you that we would not neglect his academic studies, but at this stage, Stuart is ready to find out just how far he can go as a footballer.

I know this is a big step for you and for Stuart himself. You will want to think about the future and talk to other people about the best thing to do. I am enclosing a brochure which tells you a little about what Stuart might expect as an Academy scholar at Manor Park. If there are any other questions, do give me a ring at the club.

Hope to speak to you soon.

Yours sincerely,

Derek Hardaker

Derek Hardaker (Academy Director)

Team Talk:

- How do you think Stuart's mum felt when she read the letter?
- Think of a football-related phrase to describe how Stuart felt.

Skills Practice 1

The commas are missing from these sentences. Put them in the correct places.

a) We all hope you Stuart and your father enjoyed the afternoon.

b) As I explained the other day he would be with us as an Academy player for two years.

c) After that we would then sit down with the first team Manager Mick Diamond to talk about the future.

d) One or two other clubs including Manchester City have been in touch with you.

e) We would not neglect his academic studies but at this stage Stuart is ready to find out just how far he can go.

Skills Practice 2

Find words in the letter opposite that match these three different ways of pronouncing 'ch'.

a) charm

b) character

c) chivalry

Write down six Premier League and Championship teams with 'ch' in their names.

Manager's Message

A comma gives a pause or breath in a complex sentence. Commas are not needed before the word 'and' in lists.

Game On

Answer these questions with full sentences.

1. What did Stuart's grandad talk to Mr Hardaker about at the match?
2. When would Stuart start at the Academy?
3. Does this offer mean that Stuart will play for the Shelby Town first team? Explain your answer in a sentence.
4. What is the meaning of the phrase 'a real prospect'?
5. How do you think Stuart's headmaster would respond to this offer?

http://www.shelby.premiumtv.co.uk/

Logon Contact A Creative BBC NEWS | ... Front Page Demon Inter...Mail: Login eBay UK – T...Marketplace

Shelby Town FC

- Home
- News
- Manager's page
- Fixtures
- Match reports
- Online shop
- Contact us

TRIAL DATES ANNOUNCED FOR NEXT SEASON'S ACADEMY PLACES – ALL ENQUIRIES WELCOME!

FA YOUTH CUP ROUND 3 v NOTTINGHAM FOREST

VENUE: CITY GROUND, NOTTINGHAM Kick-off 7pm

Shelby Town Team: Bell; Whitfield, Mullins, Opara, Hanlon; Bangui, Evans, Pittfield, Moore; Dolan, Harper. Subs: Mitchell (GK), Riordan, Banfield-West, Majali, Neophytou

FT: Nottingham Forest 0 Shelby Town 1

90.00 Goal kick taken long by Bell (Shelby T)

89.20 Shot by Franks (Nottm F), left-footed from left side of penalty area (12 yards), over the bar

88.15 Foul by White (Nottm F) on Dolan (Shelby T). Direct free kick taken right-footed by Riordan from own half, resulting in open play

87.00 Defending throw-in by Whitfield (Shelby T)

86.10 Cross by Cooke (Nottm F), resulting in open play

84.30 **Substitution**
Shelby T substitution: Harper replaced by Riordan (tactical)

83.20 Free kick crossed left-footed by Nixon (Nottm F) from right channel, clearance by Mullins (Shelby T)

82.00 Booking
Foul by Harper (Shelby T) on Thomsen (Nottm F). Harper (Shelby T) booked for unsporting behaviour

81.10 Defending throw-in by Hanlon (Shelby T)

80.20 Attacking throw-in by White (Nottm F)

79.00 Foul by Harper (Shelby T) on Hussein (Nottm F). Free kick crossed right-footed by Hussein (Nottm F), clearance by Opara (Shelby T)

77.50 **GOAL – Dolan (Shelby T)**
Nottingham Forest 0 – Shelby Town 1
Goal by Dolan (Shelby T) right-footed (bottom-left of goal) from centre of penalty area (12 yards). Assist (pass) by Moore (Shelby T) from left side of penalty area

Team Talk:
- Why is the text in reverse time order?
- How does live text commentary help you to visualise the game?

Skills Practice 1

Write these commentary notes as complete sentences.

a) Attacking throw-in by White (Nottm F)
b) Goal kick taken long by Bell (Shelby T)
c) Shelby T substitution: Harper replaced by Riordan

Skills Practice 2

Rewrite this section of the commentary as a paragraph describing the goal.

77.50 GOAL – Dolan (Shelby T) Nottingham Forest 0 – Shelby Town 1 Goal by Dolan (Shelby T) right-footed (bottom-left of goal) from centre of penalty area (12 yards). Assist (pass) by Moore (Shelby T) from left side of penalty area

Rewrite this description of play as a live commentary.

The midfielder was already man of the match when in the 89th minute, he strode up to rocket home a free kick ensuring victory.

Game On

Answer these questions with full sentences.

1. Were Shelby Town playing at home or away?
2. Who scored Shelby's goal?
3. Why was Harper substituted?
4. Who was playing in goal?
5. Were Shelby Town playing an attacking game or a defending game during this part of the commentary? Give a reason from the text for your answer.

Match-day programme

Young Shelby Town side bows out of Youth Cup

'It was a real disappointment on the night, but our lads can be proud of what they have done this year.'

That was the opinion of Academy Director Derek Hardaker after watching our youngsters go down 2-0 here at Manor Park in the FA Youth Cup 5th Round.

'Liverpool are a very good side,' said Hardaker, 'and you have to remember we had a team made up, for the most part, of first-year scholars. They can only improve. I think Liverpool might go on and win the competition this year. But I'm sure that, if we drew them again next season, we'd give them an even better game than we did last Thursday night!'

For 60 minutes, the Town youngsters more than matched their Premiership opponents. The nearest either side came to scoring in the first half was when Stuart Dolan's close-range header crashed against the post. Once Donovan had given them the lead on 70 minutes though, turning sharply to fire past Town keeper Frank Bell, the favourites always looked in control. The scoreline was tough on Town. Donovan added his and Liverpool's second just before the final whistle.

Derek Hardaker, who watched from the main stand alongside Mick Diamond, was also pleased with the turnout from Town supporters:

'Having nearly 5,000 at Manor Park for the game was a real thrill for the boys. It gave them a taste of the big time, if you like, and those supporters got a taste of what's to come, too. That side can stick together, as second years, for next season's FA Youth Cup. Who knows? We might even see one or two of them involved with the first team before too long! I know Mick was impressed with what he saw from our lads on the night!'

Both the under-17s and under-19s had games this morning in their Academy leagues. Listen out before kick-off against Stoke this afternoon. We'll have the scores for you at around ten to three. And you'll be able to see highlights, as always, on the website at shelby.premiumtv.co.uk. Thanks again for your support for the boys here last Thursday night!

Dolan's close-range header crashed against the post.

The manager was impressed!

Team Talk:

- Use the comic strip to retell the content of the text. Try to use as much detail as you can remember.
- How much do you know about your favourite team's youth side?

Skills Practice 1

Write two meanings for these words, one in a football context and one in a different context.

a) match
b) lead
c) fire

Skills Practice 2

Write two sentences for the words in Skills Practice 1 that use them in:

a) a football context
b) a different context.

Find the words in this paragraph that are homonyms.

The referee points to the mark. The crowd watches silently. They see the striker miss. The final result is a draw.

Write a sentence for each word to demonstrate a different context and meaning.

Game On

Answer these questions with full sentences.

1. Who was quoted in this programme page?
2. How long had the teams been playing before someone scored?
3. Why would it have been thrilling for the team to play in front of the crowd?
4. Why does Mr Hardaker think one or two players might be seen in the first team?
5. Explain why the final scoreline was 'tough on Town'.

May 2005

4 Monday

A fantastic day, but a terrible day as well. We all had meetings with Mr Hardaker today. The good thing was that he said everybody at the club really rated me. I need to work harder on the physical side and they are going to talk to Mum about a special diet to help me build my upper body strength. He has talked to Mick Diamond about me and reckons I might even get on the bench with the first team next season if I keep working hard!

I was chuffed. I rang Mum straight away and told her. Grandad was there as well. He came on the phone and he said, 'Well done.' But then he said, 'Remember, Stuart, you haven't done anything yet, this is just the start.' I know he's right. I was standing in the car park thinking about it when my best friend at Shelby, Tony Moore, came out. Tony is a second year and I know him from Dynamos days.

I ran up to him and told him what Mr Hardaker had said about maybe getting on the bench next season. Tony just looked at me and said, 'I hope so. Good luck.' I could see he was down but I couldn't believe what he told me. He had a meeting with Mick Diamond and Mr Hardaker that morning and they told him they were letting him go. They don't think he is going to be a first-team player, so it's best for him to look for a club somewhere else. Town couldn't offer him a contract.

They said they would try to help him find another club, maybe in League Two or the Conference. I could see in Tony's face he didn't know what to do. He was going to go home and speak to his parents about it. It's a horrible thing to hear, and maybe Tony will think he shouldn't bother with football now. I told him he had to keep going and that he would get another chance. He said he'd come round and watch the England game on telly at my house tonight. I just hope he turns up. This is when you need your mates, isn't it?

Team Talk:
- What was good about Stuart's day and what was bad?
- Describe a bad day you have had.

Skills Practice 1

Use *so* or *but* to join these clauses and make one sentence.

a) I was chuffed. I rang Mum straightaway and told her.
b) I felt very pleased for myself. I felt sorry for Tony.
c) I could see he was down. I couldn't believe what he told me.
d) I invited him to watch the match at my house. He might not come.

Skills Practice 2

Change the reported speech in these sentences into direct speech by adding speech marks. You will have to make some other changes too.

a) Mr Hardaker said everybody at the club really rated me.
b) They said they would try to help him find another club.
c) I told him he had to keep going.
d) He said he'd come round and watch the England game at my house tonight.

Add the correct punctuation to this sentence.

We have been speaking to players said the Blues first-team coach and there has been a fantastic response

Game On

Answer these questions with full sentences.

1. What was Mr Hardaker going to talk to Stuart's mum about?
2. What did Mick Diamond and Mr Hardaker say to Tony?
3. Why might Tony not bother with football any more?
4. Why did Stuart say, 'This is when you need your mates'?
5. Describe Stuart's mixture of emotions.

SHELBY TOWN FC U-19 Schedule

Pre-season tour August 1 – August 7

Games v Aberdeen U-19 (Aug 2), Dundee Utd U-19 (Aug 4), Hearts U-19 (Aug 6)

Monday Aug 1

08.30: **Breakfast** available at training ground until 10.00.

10.30: **On time, please!** Travel to airport for **BA flight to Aberdeen.**

14.30: Arrive Aberdeen. Travel to **Holiday Inn Aberdeen**. Meal on arrival at hotel.

17.00: Training at **University Playing Fields** followed by team meeting.

19.00: Meal and reception at **Aberdeen FC (Pittodrie Stadium). All players to attend!** Derek Hardaker to address dignitaries as discussed re 'Youth Development'.

Tuesday Aug 2

10.00: Training at **University Playing Fields**. Meal at hotel. Rest at hotel, team announced.

15.00: Travel to **Pittodrie Stadium.**

17.00: **Aberdeen FC U-19 v Shelby Town FC U-19.**

Wednesday Aug 3

09.30: Breakfast at hotel. Travel by coach to Dundee.

12.30: Arrive **Best Western Queens Hotel, Dundee**. Meal followed by team meeting.

16.30: Training, **Gussie Park** facility (*NB Artificial surface, rubbers needed*).

Thursday Aug 4

10.00: Light training, **Tannadice Stadium.**

12.00: Return to hotel. Meal. Team meeting.

17.00: Travel to **Tannadice Stadium.**

18.00: **Dundee Utd U-19 v Shelby Town FC U-19.**

Schedule continues overleaf. Do not lose this!!

Team Talk:
- Why have different fonts been used to write the schedule?
- When is it useful for your team to have a schedule?

Skills Practice 1

Divide these words into syllables and practise spelling them.

a) stadium
b) holiday
c) university
d) arrival
e) announcement
f) rubbers
g) development

Manager's Message
When dividing a word into syllables, double letters are always split, e.g. *foot/bal/ler.*

Skills Practice 2

Write your own definition of these words in the text, then use a dictionary to check them.

a) reception
b) dignitaries
c) artificial
d) address
e) announced

Write a football-related definition for the underlined words.

The squad has been rotated in recent weeks but the final line-up is now confirmed.

Game On

Answer these questions with full sentences.

1. How long does the pre-season tour last?
2. How is the team going to travel?
3. Look at the information for 19.00, Monday 1st August. Why do all players have to attend?
4. On which days does the team not have a match?
5. Where in Great Britain is the tour taking place?

Match-day programme

Reserves and youths in focus

Every match day, we bring you news from behind the scenes at Shelby Town. This season, we have a new feature, 'Reserves and youths in focus'. In each issue of the match-day magazine, we'll be profiling a young player who we hope will be part of Mick Diamond's first-team plans before long. We're kicking off the series today with a look at a local lad who's already made a name for himself around Manor Park: promising teenage striker, Stuart Dolan.

Every fan likes to see a home-grown player come through the ranks. It's even better when that player makes no secret of being a fan of the club himself! Stuart Dolan was watching Shelby Town long before he ever dreamt of playing for us. He reckons his family brought him to Manor Park for the first time when he was just four years old!

Stuart has just started his second year as a Town Academy scholar. He has three goals to his credit already this season, starring for our under-19s during the pre-season tour of Scotland. That's no surprise to anybody at Manor Park, though. Dolan has been hitting the back of the net ever since he started playing football in the Leeside Schools under-12 League.

Academy director Derek Hardaker has high hopes for Dolan: 'Stuart reminds me a bit of Michael Owen,' he says. 'He's not the biggest or the strongest, but he's quick. And he's got that knack of being in the right place at the right time around the box.'

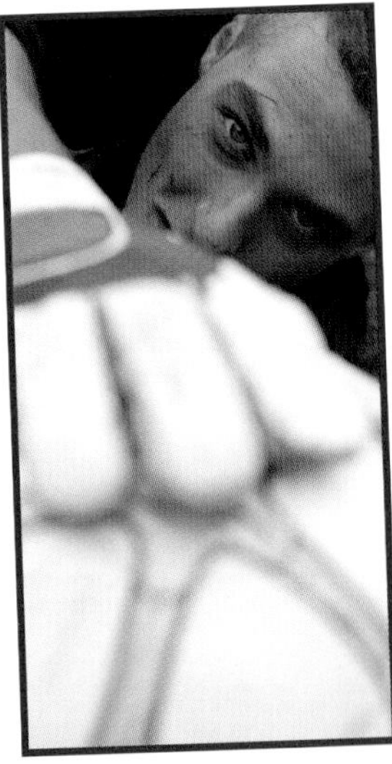

Mick Diamond knows all about the youngsters waiting in the wings, of course. He's watched the under-19s striker and likes what he sees: 'Every team needs a reliable goalscorer. Stuart still has a lot to learn when it comes to his all-round game. That ability to sniff out chances, though? You can't teach that. And young Dolan looks like he's got it!'

The boss doesn't rule out the possibility of Dolan being involved with the first team this season. For Stuart, a Town fan born and bred, that would be some kind of football dream come true. We'll watch and wait to see if it happens!

Team Talk:

- In just one sentence, say what impression this text gives you of Stuart.
- What might a player profile say about you?

Skills Practice 1

Join these shorter words together to make compound words.

a) him
b) foot
c) every
d) self
e) one
f) ball

Manager's Message
Compound words are formed by joining two words together. Sometimes a hyphen is used to help make meaning clear, e.g. 'home-grown talent'.

Skills Practice 2

Rewrite these phrases, putting a hyphen in the correct place.

a) match day meeting
b) fan club members
c) under 12s team
d) pre season tour
e) post match analysis

Find the compound words in this sentence.

Liverpool are already getting a return on the huge outlay on a new frontman from Spain just before the transfer deadline was up.

Game On

Answer these questions with full sentences.

1. How many goals did Stuart score during the pre-season tour?
2. How long has Stuart been in the Shelby Town Academy?
3. Which sentence implies that Stuart might soon play for the first team?
4. What three aspects of his play could Stuart improve?
5. Why has Stuart been chosen to feature in the programme?

Commentator: A place in the Youth Cup semi-finals at stake. And with twenty minutes to go, Shelby Town are still hanging on to that lead given to them by Stuart Dolan just before half-time, Brian.

Brian Marwood: Absolutely, Bill. Newcastle United had a spell after the break when they threw everything at Town, but I think the underdogs may have weathered the storm. United need to get the ball into the wide areas and give their strikers something to attack.

Commentator: Well, it's Shelby on the attack now. Quick break from Hanlon. And that's a great ball through for Dolan to chase. He's through. One on one with Boyle in the United goal. Out comes the keeper. And it's behind for a goal kick.

Brian Marwood: Dolan's first touch just took it away from him a bit and that was a brave dive from Boyle.

Commentator: Yes, Brian. No question but he won the ball. But Dolan's stayed down and this doesn't look good for Shelby Town.

Brian Marwood: Or for Dolan, Bill. It's his left leg, by the look of it. He's not moving and the ref's got the physio on as quickly as possible.

Commentator: In fact, they're calling for a stretcher, aren't they? A complete accident but we don't like to see this at any level.

Brian Marwood: Bill, I've just watched a replay of the incident. I hope I'm wrong but that looks like it could be a broken leg for young Stuart Dolan. His foot's got trapped under the keeper and he's fallen very awkwardly. I'm looking at Boyle's face and he's as white as a sheet. I think he knows better than anyone what's happened.

Commentator: They've strapped Dolan's legs together on the stretcher to stop any movement. And Derek Hardaker's already got a substitution ready. As you say, Brian, let's hope it's not as bad as it looks. But certainly Stuart Dolan, the Shelby Town goalscorer, will play no further part tonight. He really is in pain. We'll have to see if his team can hang on to their lead. And, as soon as we can, we'll get news on Dolan from the Shelby Town dressing room. Meanwhile, it's a goal kick to Newcastle United.

Team Talk:
- How might other team members be feeling, and why?
- What happens when one of your own team is injured?

Skills Practice 1

Write what you think these metaphors mean.

a) I'm over the moon.
b) The lads gave me everything.
c) They weathered the storm.

Manager's Message
We use metaphors as figures of speech to describe an object or an action in terms of something else.

Skills Practice 2

Rewrite these figures of speech from the text to explain what they actually mean.

a) Shelby Town are still hanging on to that lead.
b) They threw everything at Town.
c) The underdogs.

Write a sentence of your own about football and use a metaphor.

Game On

Answer these questions with full sentences.

1. How far into the game does this commentary begin?
2. Who are Shelby Town playing against?
3. How did Stuart Dolan get hurt?
4. Why did the ref call the physio on to the pitch?
5. How might Stuart's injury affect play for the remainder of the match?

February 2006

21 Wednesday

It's driving me mad! I go into the training ground for treatment after classes with the other lads. We're in the dressing room together getting kit on but then, when they go out to the pitches to play, I go down to the medical room for treatment. Then two hours in the gym on my own, working at keeping fit and building the muscles in my leg up again.

Everybody's been great. Jim Fearn, the physio, is top man. He's always positive. He makes sure I do everything I'm supposed to and then a bit more! The lads ask how I'm doing. They take the mickey out of me, saying I spend most days with my feet up indoors while they're running around in the freezing cold. Even Mick Diamond comes into the gym and says hello sometimes. But it's like I'm on the outside, not really part of what's going on.

I still remember the look on the doctor's face when they took me into hospital in Newcastle. I asked him how bad the break was and it was as if he didn't really want to tell me. He just said, 'We'll get you straight in and get it pinned. We can think about the future later.' It's weird. It didn't hurt really when it happened, but by the time I got into hospital, the pain was so bad I was sick to my stomach.

When I came round after the op, Derek Hardaker was still at the hospital; everybody else had gone back to Shelby. He said that before the operation they hadn't been sure if they'd be able to get the bones to knit properly. That could have been the end of me as a player before I'd even started!

Funnily enough, that's what keeps me going now. I know it could have been worse, a lot worse! What would I have done if they'd told me I was finished? I think about that every time I get fed up with the rehab work and the hours in the gym. I'm not going to waste this: I've got to make the most of my chance.

Team Talk:

- Look at the tense of each paragraph. Why are paragraphs 1, 2 and 5 written in the present tense?
- Have you been injured playing football? How did you recover?

Skills Practice 1

Change these present-tense verbs into the past tense.

a) I spend
b) They go
c) He makes
d) They take
e) It's driving
f) Mick Diamond comes and says

Manager's Message
Diary entries usually recount past events and use past-tense verbs. They can contain comments about the events written in the present tense.

Skills Practice 2

Change these past-tense verbs into the continuous present tense.

a) He played
b) He drove
c) I went
d) It was postponed
e) I scored

When might you use the present tense and the continuous present tense in a football context?

Manager's Message
The present tense can take two forms: *I run* and *I am running. I am running* is called the continuous present tense because the action is continuing for a while.

Game On

Answer these questions with full sentences.

1. When the other lads go out to the pitches, where does Stuart go?
2. Why does Stuart spend two hours in the gym on his own?
3. Why does Stuart say, 'It's like I'm on the outside'?
4. How have Stuart's team-mates responded to his treatment?
5. Reread the first and last paragraphs. Write a sentence to describe Stuart's state of mind.

http://www.shelby.premiumtv.co.uk/

Logon Contact A Creative BBC NEWS | ... Front Page Demon Inter...Mail: Login eBay UK – T...Marketplace

Shelby Town FC

Home
News
Manager's page
Fixtures
Match reports
Online shop
Contact us

TRIAL DATES ANNOUNCED FOR NEXT SEASON'S ACADEMY PLACES – ALL ENQUIRIES WELCOME!

Injury Latest: Dolan's Best Foot Forward

Our reporter, Sandy Lane, has been up at the training ground to get the latest on our injured players. She caught up with Academy scholar Stuart Dolan in the gym yesterday afternoon.

Sandy Lane: How's the leg feeling, Stuart? Those look like pretty heavy weights you're working with!

Stuart Dolan: Yeah, they are! I'm glad you're here so I can stop for a minute!

Sandy: What are the medical team saying about you getting back?

Stuart: I think Jim Fearn is pretty happy. He says young players always mend more quickly, but maybe that's just a way of keeping me positive. I've just started doing a bit of running this week, though. It's pretty sore afterwards and I have to ice it to get the swelling down. But Jim says that's normal. Unless anything else goes wrong, he reckons I might be able to try kicking a ball in a couple of weeks.

Sandy: So you might be ready for the under-19s before the end of the season?

Stuart: Oh, I don't know. More likely I'll have to keep working on my own for the summer and then, maybe, I'll be ready for pre-season with everybody else in July.

Sandy: Great news for you that Mick Diamond has already said he's going to offer you a pro contract to keep you at Manor Park.

Stuart: Yeah, fantastic. That's kept me going these last couple of weeks. I can't wait to get back!

Sandy: Have you been watching the first team in action?

Stuart: Oh, yes. Now I'm off the crutches, I come to all the home games. I was a Town fan a long time before I was a Town player, remember!

Sandy: And do you think we'll do it?

Stuart: What? Promotion to the Premier League? I don't see why not!

Sandy: Good luck, Stuart. Thanks for talking to Shelby TV.

Team Talk:
- What question would you ask Stuart in this interview?
- Which TV presenter would you like to be interviewed by, and why?

Skills Practice 1

Rewrite this passage, filling in the missing speech verbs without using *said*.

'How's the leg feeling, Stuart?' _____ Sandy.
'Those look like pretty heavy weights,' she _____.
'I'm glad you're here so I can stop for a minute!' _____ Stuart.

Skills Practice 2

Write a list of ten verbs you can use instead of *said*.

Use two of these speech verbs to complete this dialogue.

added *stated* *declared*

'This coming season will be challenging,' _____ the Aston Villa coach. 'We've been hit badly by injury,' he _____. 'But we can overcome these trials by hard work.'

Game On

Answer these questions with full sentences.

1. Where was Stuart when he was interviewed?
2. What does Stuart need to do after running?
3. Why will Stuart keep working through the summer?
4. What effect does Mick Diamond's offer have on Stuart?
5. Write a sentence to say what is happening to the Shelby Town first team.

Commentator: We've brought you the drama of 90 minutes, extra time and penalties here at Wembley. Coming up next on BBC Radio Leeside, it's all the hits and your requests with Simon Lederman through till ten. But before we hand over to Simon, let's soak up what's happened this afternoon. Bill North has been our summariser at the Championship Play-off Final today. Bill, you played for Shelby Town in the lower divisions for years. Did you ever think you'd see the day Town would battle their way up into the Premier League?

Bill North: Doug, it's a fantastic achievement for everybody at the club. I'm so chuffed for Dave Morgan. The skipper sticking in the winning penalty; you couldn't have written it better, could you? Mick Diamond's done a terrific job since he arrived at Manor Park. When I was playing, you'd never have imagined a day like this, even though we won promotion from the old Third Division in my time. But these lads? They deserve it. They've worked hard all season and this is their reward.

Commentator: Wonderful scenes away to our left. Thousands of Town fans singing and waving their colours! And look, Bill, Mick Diamond's got all the backroom staff to come out onto the pitch to join the celebrations.

Bill: That's a great touch. But that's Mick Diamond all over. He's got a real family thing going on at Shelby Town, hasn't he? Look, all the youth players have made their way down from the stands in their club blazers. I wonder if any of them will play Premier League football next year.

Commentator: Derek Hardaker, the Academy Director, thinks very highly of them, Bill.

Bill: He does, Doug. There's young Stuart Dolan. Good to see that lad up and about again. There was real concern about his future when he broke his leg after Christmas. But there he is, jumping up and down with his team-mates. Looks like the leg's mended now!

Commentator: Well, if you're a Town fan, you'd have to be jumping for joy. The boys will be in the Premier League next season. They've won 4-2 on penalties here at Wembley. Congratulations to them. Thanks to you, Bill. And to everyone listening. Simon Lederman's coming up next on BBC Radio Leeside, right after the news.

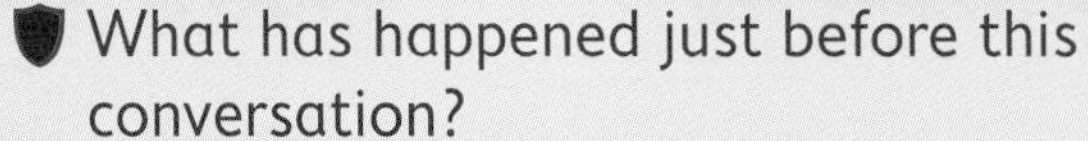

Team Talk:

- What has happened just before this conversation?
- At a match, how do you celebrate your team winning?

Skills Practice 1

Write the correct *-tion* or *-sion* ending.

a) promo
b) congratula
c) celebra

Change the above nouns into verbs, e.g. the noun *conversation* comes from the verb *converse*.

Skills Practice 2

Change these nouns into verbs.

a) division
b) possession
c) conversion

Practise spelling the nouns and verbs using Look Say Cover Write Check.

Correct the spelling mistakes below.

The players' friends and relasions were invited to a big celebrasion following their promosion to the Premier League.

Game On

Answer these questions with full sentences.

1. Who did Bill North play for?
2. What is the name of the player who scored the winning penalty?
3. Why does Bill think Stuart's leg has mended?
4. What does the commentator mean by saying Mick Diamond has a 'real family thing going'?
5. How do commentators for a radio broadcast know what is happening during a match?

Stuart knocked on the door of Mick Diamond's office. He could feel the sweat cooling on his face. He'd just finished training. The physio, Jim Fearn, had told him the manager wanted to see him.

'Come in!'

Stuart took a deep breath and stepped into the office. Mick was at his desk, scribbling away on a form.

'You wanted to see me, Gaffer?'

'Yes. Stuart. Sit down, son. Look, I wanted to let you know what's going on. You've done really well in pre-season. The leg feels okay?'

'I don't even think about it, Gaffer. A little bit stiff in the morning, but it's nothing. I feel great.'

'You're looking great, too, son, and if we were still in the Championship, I'd be looking to chuck you straight into the team.'

Stuart could feel his cheeks burning a bit. He couldn't believe what Mick had just said.

'But this is the Premier League. There's so much at stake for the club, and I haven't got time to wonder about where goals are coming from. I've signed a Nigerian international by the name of Dotun Odegbame and I'll be starting him up front against Liverpool in a fortnight's time.'

'That's fine, Gaffer. Thanks for telling me.'

'I just didn't want you to get the idea that I didn't think you were good enough. You are. But I can't afford to rush you at this level. You'll learn from the new bloke. Train with him; maybe play alongside him eventually. But, to start with, I've got to go with experience. Okay? You're going to be part of the future here, Stuart. Don't worry about that. Now go and shower and get changed, eh? And shut the door on your way out!'

'I will. And thanks, Mr Diamond. All I need to know is where I stand. I'll wait as long as I have to.'

Stuart closed the office door behind him and let out a deep breath. That's a great manager, he thought. He's just told me some bad news, but he's made me feel like it's the best news I've ever had!

Team Talk:

- How do you know who is speaking each time? What other ways can you tell readers who is speaking when you are writing?
- If your team manager wanted to see you, what would your first thought be?

Skills Practice 1

Look through the text and find eight words with the long 'a' vowel sound. Group them according to their spelling patterns, for example:

/ai/	training,
/ay/	
/ea/	
/a/	stake,

Skills Practice 2

Find a word in the text with the spelling *ign*.

How many words can you think of with *ign* spellings?

Write a list and practise spelling them using Look Say Cover Write Check.

How many ways of spelling the long vowel 'i' can you find in this sentence?

The home fans at last night's United v City match were delighted by the full-time score.

Game On

Answer these questions with full sentences.

1. Who told Stuart to go and see the manager?
2. Which team will Dotun Odegbame be playing against in his first match?
3. Why do you think Stuart took a deep breath before going into the office?
4. How might Stuart benefit from Dotun joining the club?
5. Why do you think Mick Diamond told Stuart he would not be playing in the first team yet?

Match-day programme

Reserves and youths in focus

Fulton impressed by strength in depth

The Shelby Town reserve team came through its stiffest test of the season so far last Wednesday night. The boys were up against a very strong Fulham XI. The visitors ran out 2-1 winners but were pushed all the way by a Shelby side full of Academy boys and first-year pros.

Fulham had several first-teamers returning after injury on show: Moritz Volz, Brian McBride and Clint Dempsey all started the game. The Shelby youngsters started the stronger, though, on a wet and windy evening. Evans and Pittfield took control of midfield and it was no surprise when Town took the lead. On 20 minutes, Majali swung the ball into the Fulham area. Dolan stole into space in front of his marker, and his flicked header beat Portuguese under-21 keeper Ricardo Batista from ten yards out.

It wasn't until the second half that Fulham's experienced team started to assert themselves. Danny Murphy's free kick levelled things up just after the hour. Five minutes from time, Bouazza broke clear of the Town defence and planted a low shot past Frank Bell. Coach Tommy Fulton was delighted by what he saw:

'It's not always easy working with reserve team players. But this group are great. Maybe that's because so many of them have been together for a while now. Half this team were in our FA Youth Cup sides last season and the season before. We're playing more experienced teams and the lads are challenged by that. What they've got, though, is a togetherness that you don't often see in reserve team football.

'I talk to the boss regularly and he knows how highly I rate some of these boys. You never know for sure if they're good enough until they get a chance in the first team. But you look at our goal tonight, for example: Ben Majali's pass and Stuart Dolan's finish. Premier League quality. I don't think those lads would let anybody down.'

Team Talk:

- Why do you think it is not always easy for the coach to work with reserve players?
- What effect does playing a better side have on your team?

Skills Practice 1

Choose the correct comparative form to complete these sentences.

a) Dolan is the _____ player on the team.
younger/youngest

b) Evans and Murphy ran for the ball but Murphy was _____
faster/fastest

c) Shelby played well but Fulham were the _____ team.
stronger/strongest

d) Out of the whole team, who is the _____ player?
better/best

e) The second half seemed _____ than the first half.
longer/longest

Skills Practice 2

Write the correct comparative form for each adjective.

a) beautiful
b) heavy
c) careful
d) difficult
e) tricky
f) breakable

Manager's Message
When comparing two things we add the suffix *-er*, or *more* (e.g. *more expensive*). When comparing more than two things, we use the suffix *-est*, or *most* (e.g. *the most expensive*).

Game On

Answer these questions with full sentences.

1. Who was the reserve team playing?
2. Which team was in the lead at half-time?
3. What is the difference between the Academy boys and the first-year pros?
4. Explain the meaning of 'Dolan stole into space in front of his marker'.
5. Why was the coach delighted by what he saw, even though the team lost the match?

December 2006

4 Friday

What a night! It came as a complete surprise as well! First team and reserves all trained together this morning and then Mick Diamond named the team for the Carling Cup game against Sheffield United. I thought I was hearing things when he read out the list of substitutes: 'And Stuart Dolan.' To be fair, the gaffer said at the start of the season that I should be ready if my chance came along. I still couldn't believe it!

Just to be involved tonight was fantastic: being in the dressing room with the senior players, listening to the team talk, running out to warm up in front of nearly 20,000 people at Manor Park. I spotted Mum and Grandad up in the stand and gave them a little wave. Felt a bit stupid doing it, but I couldn't help myself! I just felt so proud!

The game was excellent. We're playing so well at the moment and we deserved to go through. Hanging on a bit at the end, though, until Dotun got the second goal! As soon as he scored, the gaffer told me to start warming up. He shouted out: 'Well, you're here. You might as well earn your win bonus, son!'

I was jogging up and down the touchline, waiting for the ball to go dead. I had my tracksuit off and everything. I could see the gaffer talking to the fourth official and telling him my number. Just then, though, Pierre Vert got hurt in a challenge in midfield. The physio said he ought to come off to be on the safe side, so Mickey Evans went on and I had to sit back on the bench. We'd used all our subs!

It was a bit of a let-down, I suppose. But when I saw Mum and Grandad afterwards, they were so pleased about me being in the squad at all that I cheered up straight away! All I've ever wanted to do is play for Shelby Town. And now I know Mick Diamond thinks I'm good enough. Perhaps my big moment's coming soon!

Team Talk:

- Do you think Stuart was nervous before his debut for the first team? Why, or why not?
- What is it like to be on the subs' bench?

Skills Practice 1

Look through the diary entry and find nine words with the *gh* spelling pattern, e.g. *tight*.

Write them down and practise spelling them using Look Say Cover Write Check.

Skills Practice 2

Rewrite these sentences by moving the underlined clause.

a) I thought I was hearing things <u>when he read out the list of substitutes</u>.

b) As soon as he scored, <u>the gaffer told me to start warming up</u>.

c) The physio said he ought to come off <u>to be on the safe side</u>.

Change the order of the clauses in this sentence.

Although the ref waved play on, the players continued to appeal for a handball just outside the box.

Game On

Answer these questions with full sentences.

1. Who was the first team playing in the Carling Cup?
2. What did Stuart think when he heard his name read out?
3. Why was Stuart jogging up and down? Give two reasons.
4. Why didn't Stuart go on as a substitute when Pierre Vert came off?
5. How does Stuart know Mick Diamond thinks he is good enough for the first team?

SPORT

April 19th 2007 • Shelby Gazette

SHELBY BOOST SURVIVAL CHANCES

Allenby goal takes all three points

'A huge result for us,' declared Shelby Town boss Mick Diamond, after watching his team snatch a vital win at Reading. 'We've struggled since the Carling Cup Final, to be honest. Today we got back to doing what we do best. The goal was lucky, but I think we earned the points.'

For most of the 90 minutes at the Madejski Stadium, it was backs-to-the-wall defending for Town. Skipper Dave Morgan was outstanding. He won every header and marshalled an inexperienced back four. For much of the game, a goalless draw looked like being Town's ambition.

Top scorer Dotun Odegbame is out injured. He may not play again this season. The worry at Manor Park has been that without him Town wouldn't score enough goals to avoid relegation. But they managed one against Reading.

The chance was created by Stuart Dolan, making his first appearance for the club. On as a second half substitute, his run across the penalty area unsettled the Reading defence. The ball broke to midfielder Pierre Vert. The Frenchman's shot hit Tom Allenby on the shoulder and spun up and over Federici in the Reading goal. Allenby is an experienced striker and claimed the goal, even though he hadn't known much about it.

'They all count, don't they?' he laughed afterwards. 'We knew we wouldn't get many chances today. But we knew how important it was to win the game, too. We'll miss Dotun, but young Dolan made an impact. Perhaps he can come in and be a bit of a hero for us between now and the end of the season.'

Mick Diamond didn't want to talk about his plans for Stuart Dolan: 'I wouldn't want to put any extra pressure on the lad. But if I go with two up front on Wednesday at Manor Park, then I think he's maybe done enough to deserve a start. Stuart's still got a lot to learn, but in our position we need one or two who can come in and play without fear.'

On this afternoon's showing, Stuart Dolan can expect to make his full debut against Spurs. And Shelby Town fans can expect a real battle from their team. They're still in with a great chance of avoiding the drop.

Team Talk:
- What new headline would you use for this newspaper report?
- Has your own team featured in a newspaper? What did it say?

Skills Practice 1

Add the suffixes *-ing* and *-ed* to each of these nouns.

a) declare
b) experience
c) injure
d) create
e) appear

Skills Practice 2

These words can be used as both nouns and verbs. Write two 'football' sentences for each to show them as 1) a noun and 2) a verb.

a) result
b) struggle
c) play
d) score
e) break

Change this sentence to the continuous present tense by changing the past-tense verbs to verbs with the *-ing* suffix, e.g. *is heading.*

The coach likened his heading ability to that of 'King' Denis Law and his words proved accurate as he rose to meet the cross.

Game On

Answer these questions with full sentences.

1. What are the 90 minutes of play described as?
2. How many goals were scored in the game?
3. Why did Tom Allenby claim the goal?
4. Why didn't Mick Diamond want to talk about his plans for Stuart?
5. Read Mick Diamond's words beginning 'Stuart's still got a lot to learn, but...' to the end of the sentence. What does this tell you about Mick Diamond's impression of Stuart as a player?

http://www.shelby.premiumtv.co.uk/  Google

Logon Contact A Creative BBC NEWS | ... Front Page Demon Inter...Mail: Login eBay UK – T...Marketplace

FOOTIE TALK

Home
News
Message board
Contact us

TODAY'S THREAD:

After last night's win against Spurs, will Shelby Town still be playing Premier League football next season?

Comment by ST*TILL*I*DIE
Posted 42 minutes ago

What a night! What a goal by the lad Dolan. I must admit, two months ago I thought we'd gone. But now? Now you're going to believe us: the Town are staying up!

Comment by northstandgus
Posted 37 minutes ago

Who else was at Manor Park last night? The atmosphere was fantastic. Better than Wembley! If we'd been making that much noise every home game, we'd never have been in trouble in the first place. ONE STUART DOLAN! THERE'S ONLY ONE STUART DOLAN!

Comment by ShelbyNYNY
Posted 34 minutes ago

Hey, Gus. Some of us would like to have been there! I managed to find a bar here in New York that was screening the game, though. Place was full of Spurs fans! They couldn't believe what was happening. But I was the one singing at the end, wasn't I? One more win and we'll be safe, I think. COME ON TOWN!

Comment by ST*TILL*I*DIE
Posted 25 minutes ago

If we're in the Prem again next season, you'll have to think about moving back to Shelby, mate! And what about Dolan? I thought we'd had it after the Super Eagle got injured against Chelsea. But the young lad looked like he'd been playing for the first team forever. And what a goal! Paul Robinson never even saw it!

Comment by GeordieST
Posted 23 minutes ago

Yeah. Well done, Stuart Dolan. And he's one of us, boys. Local lad and a Shelby Town fan all his life. PREMIER LEAGUE? YOU'RE HAVING A LAUGH!

Team Talk:
- Add a message to the end of the thread.
- What do fans call themselves on your club's website?

Skills Practice 1

Rewrite these sentences with the correct punctuation.

a) What a night
b) Who else was at Manor Park last night
c) I was the one singing at the end wasn't I
d) And what about Dolan
e) And what a goal

Manager's Message
Questions can begin with question words (*how*, *why*, *etc.*) or begin with verbs (*are you, did he*, etc.).

Skills Practice 2

Change these statements into questions.

a) It was better than being at Wembley.
b) Dolan scored in the last minute.
c) The supporters were all chanting.
d) The match went into extra time.
e) The goalkeeper saved two penalty shots.

Turn this question into a statement.

Are they third in the table?

Game On

Answer these questions with full sentences.

1. Who scored in the match against Spurs?
2. Where did ShelbyNYNY watch the match?
3. How can you tell when the messages were posted?
4. Why are some words written in capital letters only?
5. Who do you think is meant by 'the Super Eagle'? Give a reason for your opinion.

MATCH OF THE DAY

John Motson: Mick Diamond, manager of Shelby Town. How do you feel?

Mick Diamond: Absolutely on top of the world, mate! It was a bit nervous waiting for the other results. But now we know we're safe, it feels fantastic. Better than winning promotion!

John: And this afternoon's game itself, Mick? Newcastle United at St James' Park? Not the easiest place to come to needing a result?

Mick: No. They did their best to make things difficult for us. They're a very good team. A big Premier League team. Getting a point here just proves that Shelby Town deserve to be playing in this league.

John: And it could have been all three points, couldn't it?

Mick: Well, obviously the boys were a bit nervous first half. But I thought we looked OK. We kept our shape and quietened the crowd.

John: They didn't look too nervous after the break.

Mick: We just told the lads to believe in themselves a bit more. They've earned the right to play at places like this. And the goal showed that. We got enough players forward and when the ball broke to Tom Allenby, I thought he took the chance really well. Shay Given was never going to get to it.

John: And young Dolan was involved again.

Mick: Yeah. Stuart's done really well to spot Tom's run. But he's been great since he came into the team. The real compliment is that we've hardly missed Dotun Odegbame, even though he'll be back next week. Stuart's attitude is what Shelby Town's all about. You saw him doing his bit to help out in defence as well after they equalised.

John: Congratulations, Mick. A fantastic achievement. Shelby Town will be playing in the Premier League again next season!

Mick: Thanks John. Delighted for the players and the fans. Every single one of them deserves it! We've shown everybody that little Shelby Town are really going places now!

Team Talk:

- What do you think Stuart's mum and grandad said when they watched the interview?
- What do you enjoy or dislike about the interviews on *Match of the Day*?

Skills Practice 1

Rewrite these phrases, putting an apostrophe in the correct place to show missing letters.

a) They have
b) We are
c) You have not
d) We would not
e) Stuart has
f) The ref is looking

Skills Practice 2

Punctuate these sentences, putting apostrophes where they are needed. Write 'O' or 'P' underneath each one, to show whether it is an apostrophe of omission or possession.

a) Stuarts run onto the pitch.
b) Stuarts run left the defence scattered.
c) The stadiums roof can be opened.
d) The stadiums packed.

Punctuate the following sentence.

Evertons ground wasnt filled to capacity but the fans singing made up for it

Game On

Answer these questions with full sentences.

1. Who have Shelby Town played in their last match?
2. What does Mick Diamond compare 'feeling safe' with?
3. What does Mick Diamond mean when he says, 'We ... quietened the crowd'?
4. 'We've hardly missed Dotun Odegbame.' How is that a compliment?
5. Why does Mick Diamond use 'little' to describe Shelby Town?

May 2007

8 Monday

I didn't wake up until 1 o'clock this afternoon! Yesterday was one of the best days of my life. What a party we had to celebrate!

I knew all along that I wasn't going to start against Blackburn. Dotun was back from injury and the gaffer was right to pick him. Without his goals, up until he got injured, we would never have stayed up. He came up to me in the dressing room and said, 'Well done, Stuart. Maybe you should be playing today.' Dotun's a very good player. He's a good bloke as well. I'm glad it was him who scored the goal that decided the game.

Anyway, I got on ten minutes before the end. I don't know if Tom Allenby was really injured or not. He gave me a big wink when he came off and I went on. I couldn't believe the cheer I got. I saw Mum and Grandad up in the stand clapping along with everybody else. What a feeling!

It was amazing being on the pitch when the final whistle went. Some young lads came running on but it didn't spoil it. We had a proper lap of honour and everything. They were singing: One Stuart Dolan, there's only one Stuart Dolan! I'll never forget it. Like the best dream I've ever had: all the players smiling and laughing; the crowd applauding and waving flags.

Actually, it's been like a dream, hasn't it? All I've ever wanted to do is play football. Play football for Shelby Town. And now I've done it. I've helped keep my club in the Premier League, the hardest league in the world. And even if it all stopped tomorrow, I'd feel everything had been worth it.

The club had a big party for us and invited all the family. Mum and Grandad came. I think Mum got a little bit tipsy. She was talking to the gaffer and they were laughing and joking together like they were best mates! Grandad was quiet, though. At the end, he looked like he was almost crying. 'Stuart,' he said, 'I brought you down to Manor Park when you were just four years old. And now look! I can't tell you how proud watching you play today made me feel!'

Team Talk:

- Use the comic strip to retell the events. Use as much detail as you can remember.
- Describe the best 'football' day of your life.

Skills Practice 1

Put the speech marks into these sentences.

a) It was an amazing day, said Stuart.
b) You're on for the last ten minutes! he shouted.
c) There's only one Stuart Dolan! cried the fans.
d) I'm so proud, she whispered.
e) You helped keep us in the Premier League! said Dotun.
f) It's like a dream come true! said Grandad proudly.

Skills Practice 2

Put speech punctuation into these sentences from the text.

a) Well done, Stuart said Dotun Maybe you should be playing today.
b) One Stuart Dolan sang the crowd there's only one Stuart Dolan!
c) Stuart, he said, I brought you down to Manor Park when you were just four years old. And now look! I can't tell you how proud watching you play today made me feel!
d) The Liverpool manager spoke to reporters. We started the season well he said Now we need to keep working.

Game On

Answer these questions with full sentences.

1. Why didn't Stuart play from the start of the game against Blackburn?
2. How much of the match did Stuart play?
3. Why was it one of the best days of Stuart's life?
4. What was amazing for Stuart, and why?
5. Why do you think Stuart's grandad was quiet at the party?

Here are some examples of the different text types and media in this book. Which ones did you like best? Write your own version of one of these texts in a different style.